Latter-Day

By

Olaf Stapledon

1914

Copyright © 2013 Read Books Ltd.
This book is copyright and may not be
reproduced or copied in any way without
the express permission of the publisher in writing

British Library Cataloguing-in-Publication Data
A catalogue record for this book is available from the
British Library

Olaf Stapledon

William Olaf Stapledon was born on 10th May 1886 in Wallasey, on the Wirral Peninsula near Liverpool, in England. Stapledon attended Abbotsholme school before enrolling at Balloil College, Oxford, where he received a BA in Modern History in 1909, and then an MA in 1913.

Stapledon was a conscientious objector during the First World War and, instead of fighting, worked with the Friend's Ambulance Unit in France and Belgium between 1915 and 1919. Upon his return he completed a Ph.D. in philosophy at the University of Liverpool. His first work of prose *A Modern Theory of Ethics* (1929) was based on his doctoral thesis. The following year, Stapledon published his first work of fiction *Last and First Men* (1930), the success of which enabled him to become a full-time writer.

Stapledon had a great impact in the field of science fiction, influencing notable authors such as Arthur C. Clarke and Brian Aldiss. His novel *Starmaker* (1937) also inspired physicist Freeman Dyson to come up with the concept for what are now known as 'Dyson Spheres', a method of obtaining vast amounts of energy from a star.

Contents

The City .... Page 7

Spirit .... Page 8

Omnipotence .... Page 9

Who Art Thou? .... Page 10

Humanity .... Page 11

Men .... Page 12

Time .... Page 13

God .... Page 14

The Heavens Declare .... Page 16

My Cup Runneth Over .... Page 18

The Rebel .... Page 20

Labour .... Page 21

Strife .... Page 23

Salvation .... Page 27

Athena .... Page 29

Apollo .... Page 31

Artemis .... Page 33

Our Lady of Heaven .... Page 35

Jaweh .... Page 36

Satan .... Page 37

Christ .... Page 38

Brahma .... Page 40

War .... Page 41

Peace .... Page 44

.

The City

I went into a city to see if there be God.
The sun was hidden from my sight; the city
 roared in my ears.
The people hurried to and fro all the day long;
 their eyes were unquiet
The half of them starved, and saw death daily before
 them. The half of them were surfeited, and
 stirred up strange desires.
Things of no moment were in their minds all the
 day long. They fought one with another,
 as monkeys over a straw.
With ceremonies they made believe to be holy;
 yet they were proud of aping the wicked.
The men whetted their lust upon the women; and
 the women were weary of motherhood.
The men and women were loathsome, for they
 had forgotten love.
I said, "If there be God, has he made them so?
What part had God in the founding of this city?"
I saw that the children were marred even in the womb;
 that God assailed them with temptations while
 yet they were weak.
I saw that the good men of the city flourished not.
The city had not been founded for them.
But surely man and not God founded the city.
How shall I condemn God for the
 blunders of men?
Yet God has permitted slaughter of the innocents.
Does the Most High God delight in the sacrifice of souls?
I said in my pride, "If there be God, he shall be no God of Mine.
I will go my way, and live according as my soul wills.
I will make war upon thee, evil God. Though thou slay me,
I will contrive justice and mercy against thy will."

Spirit

But behold, the heavens around me were very beautiful. The multitude of stars smiled upon me.

The lights of the city trembled beneath me as it were in sorrow; and her murmur was music.

Peace came upon me, and exaltation; and I marvelled that I should be exalted.

I was as though some spirit within me had certain knowledge of God, declaring, "He is gentle. He is merciful."

But I looked upon the city, and rejected comfort, saying, "Nay, thou foolish imagination.

"But the spirit would not be put down. It gloried within me.

And I saw that the spirit was excellent beyond all that I called good, and merciful beyond my mercy.

And I was amazed, and said, "Surely thou only art God who dwellest in my heart. And thou rulest the stars."

Omnipotence

I went into an open place under the stars. The city lay beneath me, and her sound was subdued.

I saw that the hosts of heaven perform that which was ordained in the beginning. The city was ordained in the beginning also.

I looked into the far place beyond the stars. I hearkened to a little wind of the earth whispering among the grasses.

And a great fear fell upon me out of the heavens, because of the majesty of God.

I said, "How shall I call thee just or unjust? Thou art mighty, and I am very small.

I am weary of myself because I am so small. I am contemptible in my own eyes because thou hast ordained what I must will.

Wherefore has thou sickened this thy little earth with a fever of life? Wherefore hast thou made the swarms of men to fret upon her?

Thou hast made the heavens for thy plaything. Thou breakest the heart of man like a toy."

My spirit was dried up within me. I sat without meditation.

.

Who Art Thou?

Who art thou that dwellest in the hearts of men; and speakest
 in my heart daily, so that I call thee God?
I feel thee excellent within me. I bow down to thee in the
 secret place within me.
Thou hast made me a law, and I will keep it.
I go amongst men, thinking of thee, saying, "I will be like
 to thee; they that are like to thee are men."
Thou art beautiful, and abhorrest that which is vile. Who art
 thou that hast made thyself beautiful out of the
 sorrow of men?
Thou didst make the nations to toil, that they might bring
 thee out of darkness into light. Art thou God
 for whom the peoples suffer?
Thou are more beautiful from generation to generation.
 Shall the peoples suffer for thee daily more and more?
I rose up and cried against thee blasphemously in the world, saying,
 "I scorn thee, thou cruel God."
But thou speakest within me: I am bowed down before thee.

Humanity

The spirit that dwells in the hearts of men spoke within me, saying:
Oh my children, ye in whom I live, ye that have suffered for me
    to make me beautiful!
Think ye that I have slain my children willingly? I am not God
    who has ordained pain.
I am the Spirit dwelling in your hearts. Ye live that
    I may be beautiful.
Ye are of me, but I am greater than you. I am the Soul of All Men.
In the days of my darkness, when I knew not myself,
    I was like a child, living in a dream.
Out of the lives of the ancient multitudes I have awakened and
    found myself. And lo! I am beautiful, and yearn toward God.
God has given me a law; and I will keep it.
I will make myself perfect. I will be beautiful in the eyes of God.
I will stand before him joyful as a bride. I will be for him a bride
    or a sacrifice according to his will.
As for you, my children, my little ones, the sorrow that ye have suffered
    cannot be undone.
But the sorrow that ye have suffered shall not be wasted.
    Because ye have suffered, behold, I am.
The lives of all the multitudes are gathered in me.
    There shall no little soul be lost.
When I stand before God, the sorrow and the joy that ye have
    suffered for me shall be in my beauty. In my blessedness
    ye shall be blessed.
Therefore hearken unto me when I speak in your hearts; for I know God.
.

Men

Behold the sons of men, who sin, whose hearts are divine!
In selfishness they heap up misery upon one another; yet for love
 they die.
They are blown hither and thither like the dead leaves; yet for love
 they are steadfast.
They trample on their kindred for a little bread; yet for a vision they
 forget themselves.
Scatter gold among them, and they fall upon one another in lust.
Show them God, and behold them sons of God.
I went into the city to be with men, and to learn their hearts.
I met them in the streets and in the public places, and the Spirit
 greeted me through their eyes, even from behind their hardness of heart.
I was with them in their homes, and their hearts opened to me like
 roses, so that I am filled with the fragrance that is in men's hearts.

.

Time

Wherefore hast thou made the world that it shall die, and the heavens that they shall burn out like a flame?
What wilt thou do when the stars are all extinguished, and there is no place for life?
The sons of men have builded for themselves a house of beauty. It is continually embellished.
The last of the generations shall dwell therein and die; and the beauty that was builded shall be no more.
A lover and his beloved have met together in the evening. Evening shall return, but they return not.
The home that seemed eternal is broken up and scattered. The children remember it; they die; it is no more.
I am heavy of heart because of fleeting time, and because all things come to nought.

.

God

The voice of God spake out of his creation:
I have made a law, that is my law of beauty. I have ordained my heavens
    that they shall blossom and wither away.
The flower shall die, but the seed shall flourish. Like a flower,
    the world shall perish, but the spirit that is born therein shall love.
If the spirit has need, shall I not make other universes for her sake,
    to be ethereal according to her necessity?
As for you, oh men, out of lifelessness I made you to live.
    Out of unconsciousness I gave you the glory of thought.
Have ye fear that I will let you slip again into nothingness?
    Do ye hunger after eternity all your life long?
Be sure that if ye die utterly, it is best that ye die; and if ye live for ever,
    it is best that ye live.
For I have made you to fulfil my purpose. Nothing that is in you
    shall be lost from me.
I have made you that ye shall create love and victory. That which
    ye create I will not destroy.
That ye may be courageous, I have hidden the future from you.
    That ye may conceive the light, I have laid my hand over
    your eyes and covered you in darkness.
That ye may know hope and despair, I have tempted you with many ideals,
    even while I resist all your striving for ever.
Yea, that ye may excel in fortitude, I will harass you all the days of your life,
    and seem to defeat you for ever.
That ye may love, I have tuned you together like music, so that in loneliness
    ye fulfil not yourselves.
That ye may increase in love, I have given you the means to sacrifice;
    that ye may sacrifice to love, and know that love is best.
That ye may know the peace of love, I have set in each of you the desire
    of a dear friend; that ye may look upon each other in wonder and
    delight, and be sufficient each to another.
That ye may know the glory of love, I have spoken to you in your friend's
    voice; and in the eyes of your beloved ye have seen me.
Thus shall ye join with all my creatures in creating for me love. Its dearness

and its splendour ye shall make for me.
Thus only shall ye come into the knowledge of me. Thus shall ye love me.
In each of my stars I have set a mighty spirit to increase in beauty.
The peoples that dwell upon the multitude of my stars are beyond number.
Exalted are they who look to Sirius and Aldebaran as ye look to the sun.
There are gentle peoples who praise me out of the midst of the Pleiades.
In every part of my heaven there is life living together; and out of its
    loving a spirit is born, to be the soul of each star.
Behold, these are my ministers who do my pleasure; who yearn towards
    one another across the great abyss;
Who fill my heaven with sing, as it were a little room
    bursting with voices;
Who shall draw near together, and be one soul, creating for me
    my heart's desire.

.

The Heavens Declare

Hast thou heard the song of the heavens,
    the chorus of innumerable stars?
If thou lie out in the darkness on the bare heath
    when the music of the wind is at rest, and the
    murmur of men is very far away; if thou listen with all
    thy soul, thou shalt hear the song of the heavens.
Thou shalt know that thou art clinging to a little star that is like a
    mote flying on the storm. And the voices of the mighty shall
    be about thee.
They shall be singing a great song. They shall overwhelm thee with
harmony.
The Spirit of Man lifteth up her voice in the chorus. There were not
harmony
    without her.
Thou shalt hear her song rising beside thee as it were the song of a child;
    but the voices of the mighty shall overwhelm thee even from the heavens
    that lie beyond thy sight.
The purport of the singing thou shalt not understand; but thy soul shall be
    filled with music.
Thy soul shall respond as it were a harp answering
    to the wind. Thy soul shall be musical
    according to her capacity.
There shall no more of the harmony enter
    thee than thou canst bear; but thou shalt
    feel glory round about thee.
Thou shalt hear lamentation as of a passionate
    sorrow, that mourneth in all the regions of
    heaven;
The sorrow in which beauty shall be brought
    forth; the terror of the darkness where there
    shall be light.
Thou shalt hear triumph as of one glorying in
    his death; the triumph of spirit fulfilled.
Thou shalt hear, as it were a melody exceeding
    sweet, the truth of that which thou callest love,
    when thou feelest it a little and art exalted.
But what is thy loving to the loving of the
    heavens, whereby they are made one?
Whereby the past liveth in the future; whereby

    the future and the past are one.
The voice of Heaven is one voice, singing a
    song of praise.
The voice of Heaven is one voice, singing a
    song of love.
Heaven prepareth for her beloved. The
    beloved of Heaven is God.

My Cup Runneth Over

THOU hast set me in the midst of beauty.
What am I that I should be singled out
for joy?
The trees clothe themselves in the green colour
of spring; their branches are filled with the
song of many birds.
By day the glory of the sun flows in my veins,
filling me with content. By night the stars
callout my spirit in worship, and I am lost
among them.
In the setting of the sun and in men's works I
see beauty; in the storm and in the thrust
of a spade.
Thou hast made me to take delight in music,
whereby my spirit ascends I know not
whither.
Thou hast made me to take delight in the
thoughts of the great, the heritage of the
generations.
Thou hast made me to take delight in men and
women, and to seek the keys of their
hearts.
Thou hast made me to love. Surely she is thy
daughter whose home is my heart, for she
is like to thee.
Wherefore hast thou blessed me thus beyond
measure? What am I that I should be
singled out for joy?
I have no merit beyond my brother. Have I
stolen my brother's blessing?
He has no respite from labouring all the day
long, and the fruit of his labour he shall
not use.
The fruit of his labour is my beatitude.

Because of him I have leisure to seek
    beauty.
His eyes are blinded with toil. He is cursed
    because of me.
Why dost thou not destroy me in anger? Hast
    thou no vengeance terrible enough for me?
Dost thou lie in wait for me till the cup of joy
    be full; to dash it from me?
Rather thou hast poisoned it with shame
    and self-despising. I drink to my soul's
    death.
Shall I renounce beauty? Shall I blind myself
    that I may be as my brother?
Shall I withdraw me from pollution for my own
    soul's sake, and deny myself selfishly?
Oh, rather let me bow the head humbly before
    my brother, and say, "I am thy servant,
    who would help thee to beauty.
Because of thy toil I have known beauty.
    I will not rest until thou know her also."

.

The Rebel

Thus spake the oppressed:
What have I to do with God? What has God
    done for me?
He thrust me into the world hungry, and I
    could get no food.
He made others to surfeit, that my mouth
    might water.
He made me to desire pleasure and shun pain, and
    overwhelmed me with heavy toil and grief.
He made me to love, and to hunger for love;
    but what home for love have I?
He made me to guess that there is beauty, and
    set his favoured ones to proclaim beauty
    lest I should forget.
But the door of his heaven he fixed ajar, that
    I might hear and not enter.
And ye speak to me of worship and the joy of
    sacrifice! Wherefore should I sacrifice to you
    and to your tyrant God?
Mighty is your God, for he made the stars and
    enslaved the peoples. Loving he is not,
    for he made me.

.

Labour

I HEARD a voice of anger rising out of the city,
 the voice of many men:
Where is the oppressor? Who is it that has
 bound us to his will?
We are like a man who would tread down fire,
 but it springs up behind him anew.
Where is the oppressor, that we may throw
 him down, and cast him into the hell that
 he has made?
We have risen against one, but he vows it is
 not he; and against another, but he
 reproaches us, saying, "Friends, I am your
 friend."
Where is the oppressor, he that lurks in the
 darkness to torment us?
Is he more worthy than we, that we should
 be his slaves? Or is he a god, that we
 should be a sacrifice to him?
Is it he that put weapons into the hands of the
 first men, that they might overcome the
 beasts?
Is it he that sweated to make the earth bring
 forth in the beginning, wrestling with
 tools against the wild?
Did he pile up the wide, mouldering cities of
the dead? Is it his blood that is upon
the pyramids?
Did he lay himself down to die on the old
 frontiers, that there might be peace behind
 him?
Did he build roads and bridges with his hands?
 Did he make the corn to grow for
 innumerable harvests?
Did he cramp his back under the earth to bring

up coal and all metals? Does he die
   daily for our sakes?
It is our backs that are bent. It is we that
   toil from the beginning until the end of
   the world.
It is we that hand down an increasing inheritance
   to all the generations, making the
   earth to be a pleasant home.
We are mighty in labour. We have great
   work to do.
Who dare hinder us? Who dare squander
   what we have made?
Where is the oppressor, the devourer, the accurst?
.

Strife

SPIRIT rages against spirit. The sons of God
    contend together in long war.
The storm breaks up the trees. The storm
    casts down the strong trees gladly.
The sea has no regard for ships. He devours
    the mariners like food.
Plagues rot the peoples. The little creatures
    of pestilence revel in the bodies of men.
With mild eyes the stag beseeches the hunter;
    but the hunter will not understand.
Warriors go forth from their homes, fresh
    with kisses. They go to destroy one
    another, made glad with the prayer of
    nations.
Each host calls the sun friend, and the stars
    give heart to each on the night marches.
They rush together in battle, calling on God
    for victory. Each cries, "God is on our side."
But the one conquers and the other is swept
    away. The deed of the one flourishes,
    but the other has striven in vain.
The victor exults, saying, "The stars are jubilant
    for us." The vanquished mourns,
    "The stars weep because of our fall"
For I am my universe. Out of my own
    heaven I gather splendour, and weave
    thereof the desire of my heart.
From the midst of myself I look out upon
    my neighbour; but how shall I fathom
    what is beyond the stars?
I cannot see his heaven. He strives for what
    I scorn.
We meet together without understanding of
    one another, as it were two ships passing

in the night. We are but as meteors in
  one another's sky.
But if the desires of our hearts clash, our
  worlds are shattered together. We rush
  into conflict, crying, "God is on our side."
We gather our friends together, crying, "Help
  to resist the Fiend, lest he tear the world
  asunder, and Hell triumph."
It is so with the selfish and the unselfish,
  the wise and the foolish, the lowly and
  the mighty; with him who labours for
  his children, and him who would save
  the people.
It is so with kings and priests, warriors and meek
  men. It is so with the prophets of God.
Spirit rages against spirit; the sons of God
  call upon God to destroy his sons.
In the multitude there are innumerable longings.
  The desires of a people are like a
  host of wings that clash together striving
  to soar.
A multitude of men is as a multitude of
  worlds; and in the midst of each is a
  heart's desire.
Who shall measure the span of the minds
  of all the living; and the longings of
  all the generations?
Who shall count the sum of all striving
  since first there was desire; or tell the
  pain of all failing since the first heart broke?
The achievement of men is glorious as a
  tower reaching up to heaven; but the
  deeds that have had no fruit, and the
  striving whose fruit is bitterness, cannot be told.
It has left no trace; yet is it great as the
  host of the dead.

Is it wasted and utterly lost? Or does it live
    in some good done without knowledge?
Martyrs bear witness in the world. Their zeal gives light.
But what of him that strives in secret and
    prevails not? And of him whose heart
    is broken within him, and yet he must
    make merry?
And what of the trees overthrown by the
    tempest, and the seed that is strewn
    upon the water?
What of the mariners whose lives are cut
    short; and the soldiers whose homes are
    desolate?
What of the peoples that have destroyed one
    another; and the peoples whose spirit has
    not lived?
And what of the sacrifice that is rejected, and
    the love that is driven away?
Believe that these are of great worth! Doubt
    not that their worth is everlasting!
For spirit lives by energy and love. Out of
    suffering also blossoms the flower, spirit.
Though we utterly die and cease, spirit dies
    not. Wherefore do we live and die but
    that spirit may be?
Believe that spirit is eternal! Yea, though the
    world a thousand times prove thee that it
    dies, believe, for it is cowardly to doubt.
There is that within thee which compels thee to
    believe; so that thou shalt triumphantly
    affirm, "I know."
Behold! The wrath of spirit against spirit is
    the raging of wave against wave, wherein
    is the strength of the ocean.
The diversity of spirit, which is infinite as the

universe, is but the diversity of one soul.
The diversity of spirit is God's joy.

Salvation

"SAVE thy soul," saith the preacher. "Be that
    thy one care."
Is there then nothing more urgent for thee than
    to save thy soul? Was it for that only
    that spirit was entrusted to thee?
"Live rightly," saith the preacher, "that thou
    mayest have peace; and blessedness hereafter."
Is it for thine own comfort that thou wilt live
    rightly? With a little virtue wilt thou
    bargain for heaven?
"God seeks thee," saith the preacher. "He implores
    thee to come to him. For very love
    of thee he reaches out both hands to save
    thee."
And wilt thou turn to God in the love of thyself?
    And wilt thou love God to save thy soul?
Is it for her soul's sake that a mother loves?
    Does she deny herself that she may be
    blessed hereafter?
And what is thy soul that it is so precious
    to thee, and thy salvation that thou must
    care for it?
Thy soul is but one among the souls of men;
    and in the company of the great, what is it?
And beside the Spirit it is less than a glow-worm
    shining against the sun. In the midst of
    the living heaven what art thou beside the
    souls of stars?
Thou and all things yearn after salvation. If
    thou save thyself alone, thou hast done
    nothing.
Men, yea, and the stars, call upon thee for help.
    But thou broodest on thy soul.
If indeed thou hast a soul, forget it. Come out

from it, and enter into the hope and fear
that is greater than thou.
Sacrifice even thy soul gladly if the world need.
Or if thou canst save it, save it not to be
thine, but to be God's.

Athena

DAUGHTER of the Most High! Spirit that
 reignest in the minds of men!
Thou art that ,through which all living things
 are kin, even the highest with the lowest.
In the beginning thou didst enter into the
 waters; and there was life.
Thou didst make for thyself creatures; and
 thou dwellest as a spirit in each.
Thou didst lead the beasts towards wisdom,
 that there might be men.
Thou wert in the minds of the first peoples
 when they wearied of brutishness, when
 they opened their eyes and saw beauty.
Thou makest the peoples to conquer the earth
 and tame the lightning and understand the
 stars, that their spirits may be enlarged in
 wisdom and virtue.
Thou wilt make of mankind a noble being,
 even Humanity thy minister.
Thou dwellest in each of thy servants, to direct
 his ways.
Thou makest thy men heroes; thy women are
 high-souled.
In evil times thou enlightenest the mind with
 fortitude. Thou hast established the
 spirit in wisdom.
Thou art not dismayed by the darkness of
 heaven and the baseness of men. Thou
 understandest, and contrivest light.
For thou art a sure truth in the mind, and a
 security against dismay.
Thou art the peace whence comes faith, and
 the blessedness that can accept all sorrow.
Thou restrainest thine anger, because thou

understandest.
Thy love is calm and has few words; but it
    changes not, for thou lovest with understanding.
Thou temperest joy from excess. A quiet
    heart is thy home.
Thou art the serene sky, and the wind of the
    hills. Thou dwellest behind steadfast eyes.
Spirit, be with us lest we fall again into brutishness,
    lest we be scattered again into the dust.
Take us to be thy ministers, that we may
    spread thy good word.
.

Apollo

POET, whose song is the universe! Creator, who
    hast made the world as the expression of
    thine art!
Thou hast taken stars and space to be thy language.
    Life and death is the music of thy lyre.
From the hearts of men thou strikest thy rich
    chords. Thou soundest a melody out of
    each man's life.
Thy work is terrible and fair, for thou hast no
    aim but beauty.
Thou hast set joy to shine forth against sorrow,
    as the blue sky in the midst of the
    storm.
Thou carest not for the happiness of men. For
    beauty only hast thou care.
Thou wilt not make sorrow to cease, for tragedy
    is beautiful.
Therefore are hearts broken, even to fulfil thy
    harmony.
Therefore are souls degraded into the pit. Yea,
    even souls are destroyed.
Therefore are the nations crushed, and all the
    creatures of life swept away.
For thy universe is a great music; wherein is
    terror, darkness, and a singing melody of joy;
Wherein is strife and victory; and a haunting despair;
Wherein is love lyric, and love serene; wherein
    is love triumphant, and love overthrown
    by Time.
Thou hast struck forth thy universe in an ecstasy
    that it may perfectly declare thy thought.
Thou attainest the whole span of beauty, and
    the harmony thereof is passing sweet and wild.
Thy sign is the sun, which burns upon the sea

in his uprising, and emblazons the heaven
    with fire;
Which kindles all dark things into splendour,
    and exalts a man to cry, "Hail, God,
        my brother! "
For all who create are thy kin; and all men create;
Both the makers of song and music, and they
    that speak through colour and form;
They that contrive great books, and they that
    live fair lives;
They that mould peoples, and they that bring
    up sons to be noble.
Master! Breathe into us thy spirit, that we may
    create beauty every day;
That our lives may be as a song, that is sung in
    harmony with thee.

.

Artemis

SPIRIT! Who art purity on the white mountains,
    which inhabit the zenith with steadfastness;
Who art purity in the crescent moon, that rises
    in the dawn and is lost in the sun's light;
Who art purity in the frosty sky; and in the
    lightning also;
Who art purity in the soul, and lookest out
    from the eyes like morning.
In a world that is spirit thou art spirit excellent.
    In a world that is divine thou art
    the holy of holies.
Where all is beauty thou art that for which
    beauty strives. Where all is love it is
    thou that are beloved.
Creation aspires to thee. She exists for thy
    worship.
As for man, when thou makest his mind thy
    holy place he knows thee, and his life
    prophesies thee.
But thou dwellest apart from the multitude,
    and thy visitation is to the elect.
To him that pleases thee thou hast stooped in
    his slumber to kiss him; and his dream is
    of thee, and his desire is toward thee
    henceforth for ever.
Thou hast stood in his path on the mountain,
    or in the starlight, and he has bowed
    down in terror and joy.
For thou art terrible; and if thine elect err
    thou wilt destroy his soul.
But if he keep him pure for thee and worship
    thee with his whole heart, there is no joy
    beside his.

Goddess, dwell in us! For it is better to be
  thine than our own.
.

Our Lady of Heaven

MOTHER, who art in all life; who art the
    sweetness wherein is strength;
Who makest the maiden tender-hearted, and
    the matron steadfast;
Who fillest the mind with loving-kindness, and
    makest the heart strong to protect;
Who puttest into the trees the desire to bear
    fruit, and into the beasts joy in their young.
Thou didst make the round world to bring
    forth life, and yield her sweetness day by day.
In the beginning thou didst conceive the living
    fire of heaven; wherefore thou wilt not
    cease to give thanks.
The stars are thy children. Thou watchest
    over them with loving pride.
Thou art the present smiling upon all that is
    to come, glorying in the child that shall
    be fulfilled.
Thou art humanity our sweet mother, who
    liveth in her children's joy.
Thou art in every woman; and the hearts of
    men are not without thee.
Thou art the mild influence of the evening
    persuading men to rest.
Thou art the blue sky, that puts away our
    sorrow, as a mother laughing over her child.
Thou art a whisper that is everywhere saying
    "There is nothing to fear."
Mother, dwell in thy daughters that they may
    be like to thee; and in thy sons that they
    may know thee and do thee service.

.

Jaweh

O GOD, whose law is upon the heavens; whose
    law is not broken;
Who orderest the courses of the stars, and
    directest the rain drops;
There is nothing that errs from thy direction;
    the obedience is exact.
Thou settest thy creatures one against another,
    and awardest victory according to thy pleasure.
Thou commandest the oak tree to grow into
    majesty, that thou mayest triumph in thy lightning.
Thou makest merry in the thunder; the
    earthquake is the stirring of thy hands.
Thou hast made for thyself an enemy to war
    upon thee. Thou hast given him courage
    and a sword, that thou mayest glory in
    his fortitude.
Thou hast made man to labour; and if his
    work displease thee, thou scatterest it like chaff.
Thou hast appeared to man in splendour, so that
    he cannot forget.
Thou hast set thy precept in his heart, and if
    he err therefrom he shall die.
Thou hast given to one strength to keep thy
    commandment, and to another thou hast
    ordained sin.
To the one thou hast awarded peace even in
    sorrow. For the other thou hast set a
    fiery hell in his heart to torment him.
O God, we cannot understand thy government.
    Thy justice is not ours.
But what thou wilt, that is just. O God,
    conform our will to thine.

.

Satan

THOU who rebellest against the Almighty in
    all his dominion, scorning to be a slave
    even under him;
Who puttest bitterness into the cup of his
    victory, and laughest in his face out of Hell;
Who art for ever overpowered and never conquered;
    who hast no hope and desirest no respite.
Who hast thine own wisdom, whereby thou
    hast laid bare the treachery of the Almighty;
    and thine own virtue, which
    is to be true to the wisdom thou hast gained;
Who art God unto thyself, preserving thyself
    with a strong will.
It is thou that makest the uprooted tree to
    sprout, and the stag at bay to be terrible.
It is thou that puttest wrath into a man among
    his enemies, and into him that stands up
    one against the world.
Thou art the god of heroes, and of those who
    battle against fate.
Teach us thy wisdom that we may scorn the
    Almighty; and thy fortitude that we may
    not shrink to cast him off.
We hail thee, thou God in Man! We magnify
    thee against God in Heaven.

.

Christ

THOU lovest all things. Thou sharest all hope
and fear.
Thou bearest the pain of the whole world, and
its joy also.
Thou respectest the life of a gnat. Thou
treadest not upon the dwelling of the ants.
Thou knowest well the strength of desire. Thou
hast entered into the sins of all men.
Thou sayest to him who hates himself "Friend";
and to him who has lost heart thou imputest
courage.
Thou trustest him who will not trust himself.
Thou hast taken him to be thy minister.
Thou respectest the bitterness of him whose
work is lost, and thou sheddest sweetness
over him.
If any victor be puffed up, thou understandest
and smilest at him. Thou openest his
heart, and his pride blows away.
If any two contend, each calling his cause holy,
thou exultest with both; but into the heart
of each thou whisperest understanding of
the other.
Thou holdest out thy hand to the outcast; and
thou drawest all the peoples together.
Thou losest thyself in every man and woman.
Thou hast forgotten thyself for ever in love.
Thou hast reached beyond man's wisdom, and
thou hast come again into the faith of a
child.
Thou understandest the wisdom of the
Almighty, and thou art gladly at one
with him.
Oh thou pattern unto all men, who dwellest in

the heart of every man! Oh thou God in
Man, who knowest thyself God in Heaven!

.

Brahma

THOU everlasting, thou all-pervading, in whom
    all things have their being!
As we feel our bodies, so feelest thou earth and
    heaven. Even as our bodies are filled
    each with a life, so heaven is alive with thee.
Thou feelest the drifting of a mote in the air,
    and of light in the ether.
Thou feelest the passion of two lovers, and
    the dying of a star.
As our spirits excel over our bodies, so over the
    heaven transcendest thou.
The flesh is but a dream of the spirit, and
    creation is one of thy thoughts.
Thou art the only fact. The rest is thine imagining.
Thou dwellest in thyself for ever. Thou
    knowest thy whole self through and
    through.
The blossoming of this universe passeth not
    away. For thee all time is now.
Time is, because there is blossoming; wherein
    thou hast made beauty to be.
The soul of a man extendeth beyond the
    heavens; for thou art his soul.
The soul of a man containeth the whole past and
    the whole future; for thou art his soul.
The soul of a man containeth all souls; for thou
    art his soul.
Thou hast confined thyself in each of us, that
    thou mayest put on infinite diversity.
Behold, we bring thee each the diversity that
    thou hast willed. We long to enter into thee.

War

"COME forth, oh ye young men of all the
    nations, for the Fiend is risen against you
    to destroy!"
Who is the Fiend that is risen against us, and
    wherefore wills he to destroy?
"He is your brother, who aspires Godward;
    and he is in arms, lest ye overthrow him
    and destroy."
Wherefore should we come forth against our
    brother? We will not overthrow the
    servant of the Most High.
"Be ye then overthrown and made nothing,
    and be ye abolished from among the
    servants of the Most High!"
God commanded peace, and we will preserve it.
    In the ways of peace we serve the Most High.
"God is enshrined among you, and ye shall
    preserve him. Ye shall not meekly watch
    his temple be cast down."
So also say our brethren whom the Fiend
    possesses; yet seek we not their temple to
    cast down.
"The Fiend is risen against you, is risen against
    you! Shall the holy place of the Lord
    God be defiled?
For the land that bred you is the holy place of
    God; but the land also of the enemy is
    holy land."
We will not defile the holy lands with blood,
    and lay before God an offering of destruction.
"Arise! And overthrow the oppressor, who
    marshals your brethren against you to make you slaves."
The oppressor also marshals us. We will not,
    help him to enslave.

"Rise up, ye young men of all the nations and
    learn war, that ye may overthrow the oppressor
    from all his dominion!
The Lord God commands you to war, that the
    flame of your spirit may be kindled, that
    ye may feel God.
For the shrine of the Most High is defiled
    in you, and he will purge it with war.
Therefore put off the habit of peace, and throw
    away self, and set aside your heart's desire.
Come forth! oh ye young men! For the Lord
    God has ordained a sacrament of courage,
    that the spirit of his peoples may be born again."
Behold, then, we come forth in our millions!
    Behold, we are gathered together in nations
    of armed men!
We have put off the habit of peace, and
    thrown away self, and set aside our heart's desire.
We young men have parted from our beloved,
    whom we thought to wed.
We newly wedded shall not meet again. She
    that loves shall be left alone desolate.
Homes shall be rooted up. Children shall cry
    after their fathers in vain.
Mothers shall give up their sons. Fathers shall
    be alone in their old age.
The dead shall be a mighty host; and there
    shall be agony, and horror, and grief immeasurable.
The innocent shall be trampled under foot, and
    the victor shall be debased with bloodthirstiness.
But the peoples shall rise up, and the oppressor
    shall fall.
War music is in the air like a summons, and the
    heart beats to the drum.
Therefore let us go forth gladly even into the
    place that is Hell. Surely we will go

    singing even down into the pit.
For the Most High God is within us, and him
    we will preserve.
.

Peace

I HEARD a voice calling out of the battle,
    "Peace! let us make peace!" And the
    armed hosts answered and sighed, "Peace,
    give us Peace !"
All men and women in all the earth longed also
    for peace; saying, "We are weary, we are
    chastened, let us love one another and
    advance the spirit."
Peace shall come again. May the peoples be
    made one!
We shall gather up the threads again, even the
    threads that war cut.
Many shall come home rejoicing. Many shall
    receive back their beloved.
The spirit shall be kindled again in all men
    and women, and they shall worship together.
They shall give thanks for the new age, and for
    the victory of the dead.
And the souls of the dead shall be gathered
    into the spirit; and the spirit shall flourish
There shall be a new heaven and a new earth,
    and joy shall be again. But the dead shall
    not come back.